THE WORLD OF DINOSAURS

BY REBECCA SABELKO

TYRANNOSAURUS REX

EPIC

BELLWETHER MEDIA • MINNEAPOLIS, MN

EPIC BOOKS are no ordinary books. They burst with intense action, high-speed heroics, and shadows of the unknown. Are you ready for an Epic adventure?

This edition first published in 2020 by Bellwether Media, Inc.

No part of this publication may be reproduced in whole or in part without written permission of the publisher. For information regarding permission, write to Bellwether Media, Inc., Attention: Permissions Department, 6012 Blue Circle Drive, Minnetonka, MN 55343.

Library of Congress Cataloging-in-Publication Data

Names: Sabelko, Rebecca, author.
Title: Tyrannosaurus Rex / by Rebecca Sabelko.
Description: Minneapolis, MN : Bellwether Media, Inc., 2020. | Series: Epic: The World of Dinosaurs | Audience: Ages 7-12. | Audience: Grades 2 to 7. | Includes bibliographical references and index.
Identifiers: LCCN 2019002791 (print) | LCCN 2019003469 (ebook) | ISBN 9781618916624 (ebook) | ISBN 9781644870907 (hardcover : alk. paper) | ISBN 9781618917379 (pbk. : alk. paper)
Subjects: LCSH: Tyrannosaurus rex--Juvenile literature. | CYAC: Dinosaurs.
Classification: LCC QE862.S3 (ebook) | LCC QE862.S3 S2325 2020 (print) | DDC 567.912/9--dc23
LC record available at https://lccn.loc.gov/2019002791

Editor: Betsy Rathburn   Designer: Jeffrey Kollock

Printed in the United States of America, North Mankato, MN

TABLE OF CONTENTS

THE WORLD OF THE TYRANNOSAURUS REX

PRONUNCIATION ⚠

tye-RAN-uh-SAWR-us rex

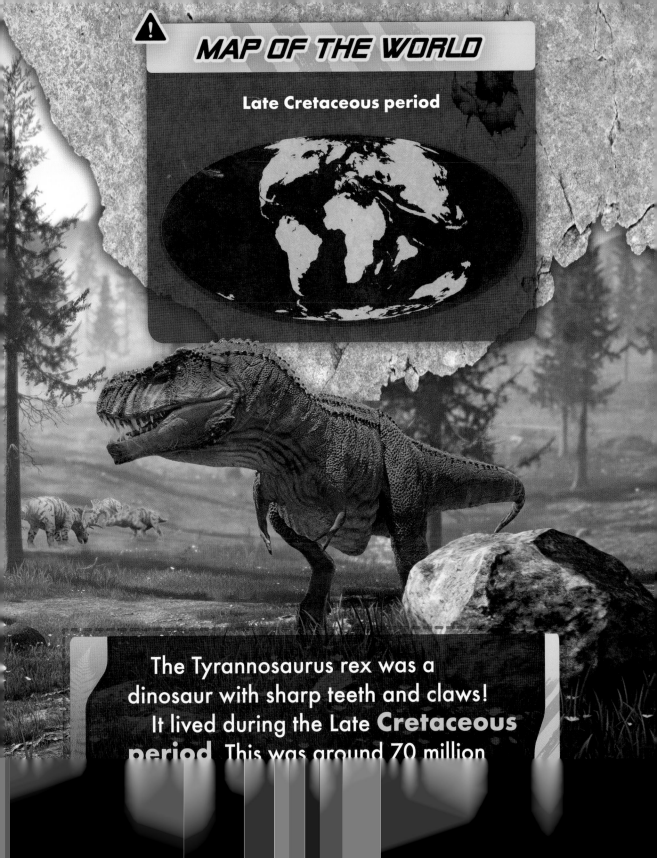

⚠ MAP OF THE WORLD

Late Cretaceous period

The Tyrannosaurus rex was a
dinosaur with sharp teeth and claws!
It lived during the Late **Cretaceous**
period. This was around 70 million

WHAT WAS THE TYRANNOSAURUS REX?

⚠️ **NAME GAME**

Tyrannosaurus rex means "king tyrant lizard" in Latin!

The T. rex walked on two strong legs. Its tail stuck out straight. This helped the T. rex keep its balance.

Advanced inner ears also kept the T. rex steady!

DIET AND DEFENSES

Scientists think the T. rex was a **predator**.
It used its size and strength to take down **prey**.
The T. rex was also a **scavenger**.
It ate any food it could find!

T. REX DIET

rotting meat

triceratops

Edmontosaurus

⚠️ BANANA TEETH

Some T. rex teeth were about the size of a banana. They were over 8 inches (20 centimeters) long!

The T. rex had wide jaws. It could crush bone with one bite! Its mouth was filled with more than 50 pointed teeth! They easily tore through meat.

Tiny arms meant the T. rex could not break its food apart. Instead, the dinosaur ate meat in large chunks. The dinosaur threw its head back to force food down its throat!

⚠ A GIANT BITE

The T. rex ate a lot. It may have been able to eat up to 500 pounds (230 kilograms) of meat in one bite!

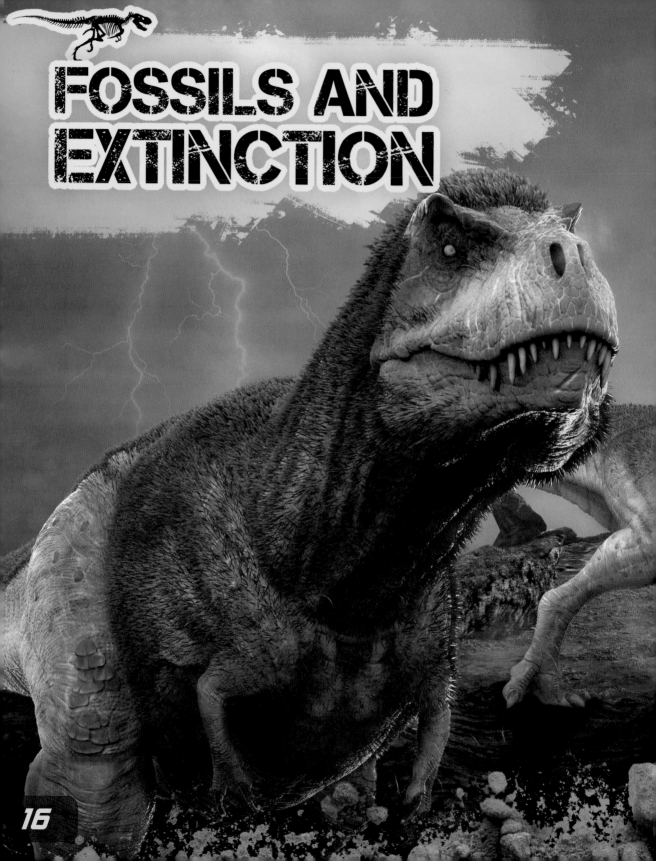

FOSSILS AND EXTINCTION

A huge **asteroid** hit Earth about 66 million years ago. The **impact** destroyed the T. rex's **habitat.** Eventually, dinosaurs went **extinct.**

⚠ LONG GONE

Dinosaurs were not the only animals that went extinct when the asteroid hit. More than half the plants and animals on Earth died out!

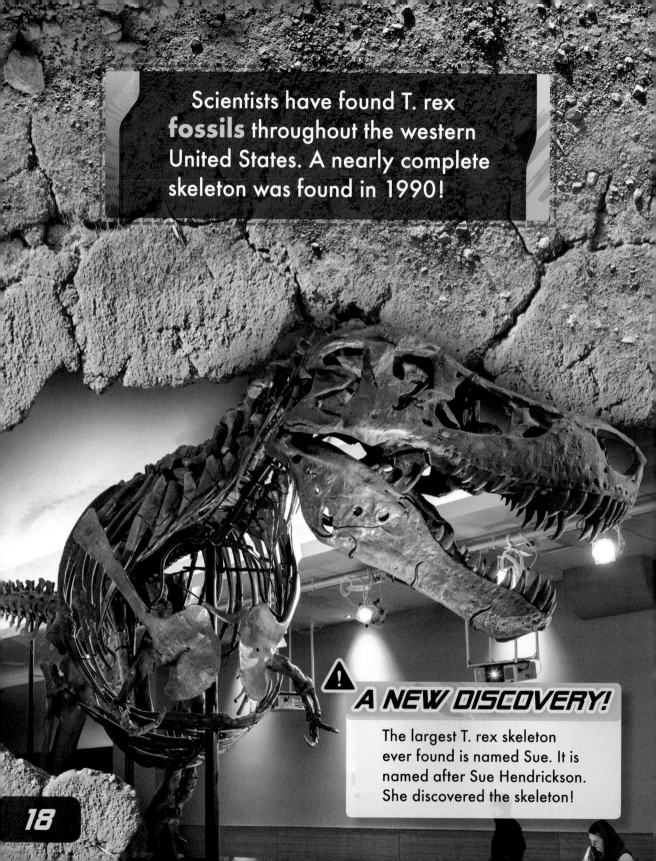

Scientists have found T. rex **fossils** throughout the western United States. A nearly complete skeleton was found in 1990!

⚠️ A NEW DISCOVERY!

The largest T. rex skeleton ever found is named Sue. It is named after Sue Hendrickson. She discovered the skeleton!

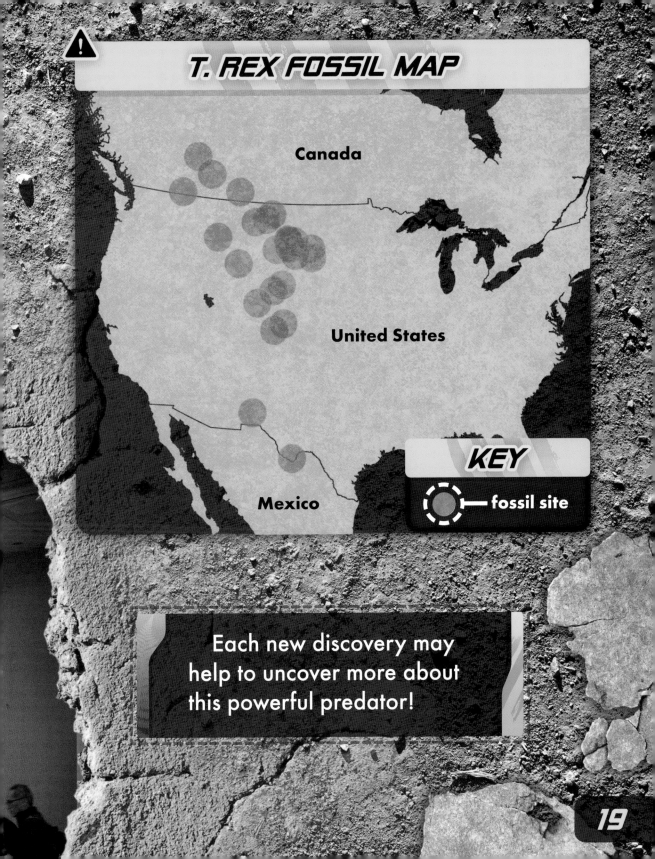

T. REX FOSSIL MAP

Canada

United States

Mexico

KEY

fossil site

Each new discovery may help to uncover more about this powerful predator!

GET TO KNOW THE TYRANNOSAURUS REX

⚠️ **FIRST FOSSILS FOUND**

1902 in Hell Creek Formation, Montana

long tail

HEIGHT 12 feet (3 meters) tall at the hip

⚠️ **WEIGHT** up to 18,000 pounds (6,350 kilograms)

LENGTH 40 feet (12 meters) long

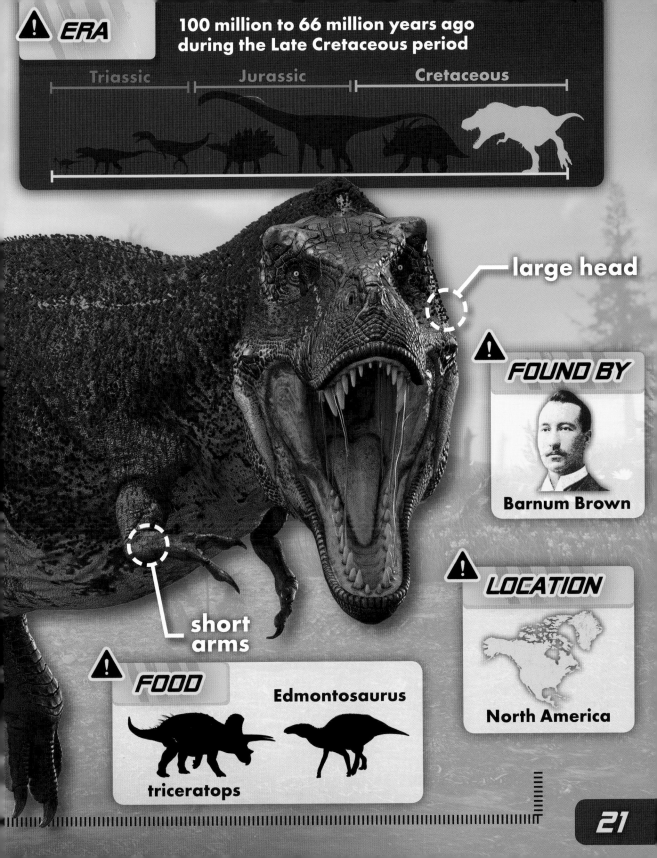

⚠ **ERA**

100 million to 66 million years ago during the Late Cretaceous period

Triassic | Jurassic | Cretaceous

large head

⚠ **FOUND BY**

Barnum Brown

short arms

⚠ **LOCATION**

North America

⚠ **FOOD**

Edmontosaurus

triceratops

21

GLOSSARY

asteroid—a small rocky object that circles the sun

Cretaceous period—the last period of the Mesozoic era that occurred between 145 million and 66 million years ago; the Late Cretaceous period began around 100 million years ago.

extinct—no longer living

fossils—the remains of living things that lived long ago

habitat—land with certain types of plants, animals, and weather

impact—an event in which an object hits another object

predator—an animal that hunts other animals for food

prey—animals eaten by other animals for food

scavenger—an animal that eats food that is already dead

TO LEARN MORE

AT THE LIBRARY

Gilbert, Sara. *Tyrannosaurus Rex*. Mankato, Minn.: Creative Education, 2019.

Sloan, Christopher. *Tracking Tyrannosaurus: Meet T. Rex's Fascinating Family, from Tiny Terrors to Feathered Giants*. Washington, D.C.: National Geographic, 2013.

Waxman, Laura Hamilton. *Discovering Tyrannosaurus Rex*. Mankato, Minn.: Amicus, 2019.

ON THE WEB

FACTSURFER

Factsurfer.com gives you a safe, fun way to find more information.

1. Go to www.factsurfer.com.

2. Enter "Tyrannosaurus rex" into the search box and click 🔍.

3. Select your book cover to see a list of related web sites.

INDEX

The images in this book are reproduced through the courtesy of: James Kuether, front cover, p. 11 (rotting meat); Herschel Hoffmeyer, pp. 4-5, 6-7, 8-9, 10-11, 12-13, 14-15, 16-17, 20-21; Gabbro/ Alamy, pp. 18-19; University of Kansas Library Archives/ Wikipedia, p. 21 (Barnum Brown).